Roadside Wild Fruits of Oklahoma

Dr. Doyle McCoy

Roadside Wild Fruits of Oklahoma

By Doyle McCoy

University of Oklahoma Press : Norman

By Doyle McCoy

Keys to the Flowering Plants of Pontotoc County, Oklahoma (Ada, Oklahoma, 1963)

A Study of Flowering Plants (Lawton, Oklahoma, 1976)

Roadside Flowers of Oklahoma 2 vols. (Lawton, Oklahoma, 1976, 1978)

Library of Congress Cataloging in Publication Data

McCoy, Doyle, 1917–
  Roadside wild fruits of Oklahoma.

  Bibliography: p.
  Includes index.
  1. Roadside flora—Oklahoma—Identification. 2. Fruit—Oklahoma—Identification. I. Title.
  QK181.M33   582'.0464'09766   79–6705
  ISBN 0–8061–1626–9

Copyright © 1980 by the University of Oklahoma Press, Norman, Publishing Division of the University. Manufactured in the U.S.A. First edition.

To my daughter, Judy, who has always been a source of support and encouragement, even from the first field trip that she made with her "Daddy."

Contents

Introduction	*page* xi	
Acknowledgments	xiii	
Color Plates	2–70	
Description and Distribution	3–71	
References	72	
Glossary	73	
Index	77	

Illustrations

Coral Vine	2	Winged Sumac	16
Yaupon	2	Smooth Sumac	16
Winter Berry	2	Skunk Bush	16
Climbing Bittersweet	4	Burning Bush	18
Wild Rose	4	Sticker Weed	18
Swamp Rose	4	Missouri Evening Primrose	18
Flowering Dogwood	6	Trifoliate Orange	20
Pencil Cactus	6	Tree Cactus	20
Prickly Pear	6	Osage Orange	20
Tree Plum	8	Mistletoe	22
Chickasaw Plum	8	Rough-leaved Dogwood	22
Thorn Apple	8	Poison Ivy	22
Southern Blackberry	10	Red Haw	24
Wild Blackberry	10	Soapberry	24
False Grape	10	Persimmon	24
Western Crab Apple	12	Common Greenbrier	26
American Holly	12	Possum Grape	26
Downy Haw	12	Summer Grape	26
Beauty Bush	14	Common Chokeberry	28
Indian Currant	14	Black Cherry	28
Prickly Ash	14	Chittam Wood	28

American Elder	30	Bush Clover	50
Pokeweed	30	Cocklebur	52
Virginia Creeper	30	Bur Apple	52
Catbrier	32	Buffalo Bur	52
Rattan Vine	32	Japanese Honeysuckle	54
Privet	32	Chinaberry	54
Red Cedar	34	Hogwort	54
White Indigo	34	Pepper Vine	56
Black Haw	34	Water Lily	56
Devil's Claw	36	Golden Currant	56
Trumpet Creeper	36	Blue Beech	58
Coral Bean	36	Ironwood	58
Ohio Buckeye	38	Red Bud	58
Sweet Gum	38	Prairie Parsley	60
Sycamore	38	Common Rush	60
Red Ash	40	St. Andrew's Cross	60
American Elm	40	Illinois Mimosa	62
Red Elm	40	Bear Grass	62
Shepherd's Purse	42	Shortleaf Pine	62
Silver Maple	42	Red Oak	64
Wafer Ash	42	Scrub Chestnut Oak	64
Bladder Pod	44	Post Oak	64
Antelope Horns	44	Sugar Berry	66
Devil's Tongue	44	Western Hackberry	66
Passion Vine	46	Button Bush	66
Common Gourd	46	Pale Purple Coneflower	68
Prairie Angle Pod	46	Button Snakeroot	68
Pecan	48	Leavenworth's Eryngo	68
Bur Oak	48	Common Dandelion	70
Black Walnut	48	Cotton Bush	70
Bur Cucumber	50	Hairy Goldenrod	70
Brown Sedge	50		

Introduction

FOREWORD

I am always impressed with the beauty and orderliness of God's universe. The fruits of Oklahoma's herbs, trees, and vines are second only to the flowers of these same plants in displaying this beauty. This book represents another in a series of guides for identifying those plants that abound along the roads of the state.

PURPOSE

This fruit guide is produced in response to many requests for such a publication. These requests have come from those who have enjoyed my two-volume publication, *Roadside Flowers of Oklahoma*. This book, like the flower guides, provides a nontechnical description of Oklahoma's plants and emphasizes use of the color plates for their identification.

METHOD OF PREPARATION

I have made periodic visits to every Oklahoma county in order to photograph the more striking and more widely distributed fruits. This has entailed much more time and concentrated study than might be imagined just by looking through the book. However, they were pleasant hours because I was learning, continuously, such things as new locations, new taxonomic characteristics, and even occasionally the discovery of a plant group that I had not observed before except in cultivation. And it is always exciting to share some of my knowledge and appreciation of these beautiful fruits with others who are interested.

The photographs were made with a thirty-five millimeter camera equipped with a close-up lens. At least one fruit to be photographed, along with additional plant parts, was arranged before a very dark background. Several shots of each specimen were made so that some option could be used in selecting the one for a plate. Since several different species occasionally produce almost identical fruits, it seemed best to limit the selection to a single representative of the group.

Descriptions, distributions, and other information are provided, so that the fruits may be more conclusively identified and enjoyed. The source of my information, provided for each species that is included, is threefold: (1) personal observations over many years, (2) discussions with other botanists and local residents, (3) published references that are listed in this book.

The scheme of organization used in this book is based on coloration of the mature fruits. One may readily observe that the fruits of Coral Vine, Yaupon, and Winter Berry are bright red. Therefore, the photographic plates representing these three species are on the same page. I believe this arrangement enhances the aesthetic value of the book. It should also provide for greater convenience in locating the illustrations for matching field specimens.

Acknowledgments

I wish to express a very special gratitude to the many members of various garden clubs of Oklahoma for their encouragement. Several of the slides, from which plates were produced for this publication, have been shown to many of these club members and their response has been very encouraging.

Also, the comments of college and university co-workers, as well as those from secondary school personnel, state and national park officials, and soil conservation personnel have been catalysts in the background for this publication.

Roadside Wild Fruits of Oklahoma

CORAL VINE
Cocculus carolinus

Moonseed Family
Menispermaceae

YAUPON
Ilex vomitoria

Holly Family
Aquifoliaceae

WINTER BERRY
Ilex decidua

Holly Family
Aquifoliaceae

CORAL VINE

These are very frail vines that climb to a height of several feet. The leaves are mostly heart-shaped with long petioles. The flowers are small, clustered, and inconspicuous. The fruits are red, single-seeded, about 1/4 inch thick, and ripen in the late fall. They usually are in compact clusters and are scarlet red. They remain attached into the winter season and provide food for several species of birds. They occur in low woodlands and thickets throughout the state. Other names are Carolina Moonseed and Red-berry Moonseed.

YAUPON

These are small trees that retain their leaves during most of the winter. The twigs are covered with short hairs. The leaves are smooth, ovate to elliptic and have wavy margins. The fruits are scattered on short stalks of the new branches. Each fruit is bright red and 1/6–1/4 inch in diameter. They mature in early fall and remain attached into the winter, when they supply food for several species of birds. They may be found in low woodlands of our eastern counties. Other names are Cassena, Emetic Holly, Appalachian Tea, Carolina Tea, and Indian Tea.

WINTER BERRY

These are small trees or shrubs. The twigs are light gray and smooth. The leaves are smooth, dark green, blunt at the apex, sharply wavy on the margins, and are always lost from the tree in the fall. The fruits ripen in the fall, remain attached into the winter months, and provide food for birds and small mammals. Each fruit is red, 1/6–1/4 inch thick, and they are clustered on short, lateral stems. They are most frequent in low, rich soils of our eastern counties. Other names are Swamp Holly, Deciduous Holly, Bearberry, and Possum-haw.

CLIMBING BITTERSWEET
Celastrus scandens

Staff-tree Family
Celastraceae

WILD ROSE
Rosa setigera

Rose Family
Rosaceae

SWAMP ROSE
Rosa carolina

Rose Family
Rosaceae

CLIMBING BITTERSWEET

These are climbing, woody vines that may reach a height of 25 feet or more. The leaves are oval, 2–4 inches long, slightly serrate-margined, and sharply pointed at the tips. The flowers are inconspicuous. The fruits are yellow to brown capsules that open in the fall to expose red, fleshy, spherical interiors. They are very conspicuous and attractive as they drape themselves over branches of available trees. They grow occasionally along streams or ravines, and are mostly eastern. Other names are Staff-vine, Fever-twig, Orange-root, and Jacob's Ladder.

WILD ROSE

These are climbing, prickly plants with woody stems that are often several feet long. The leaves are pinnately compound with three or more leaflets. The flowers are 2–3 inches broad with five, pink to white petals. The fruits are globose, reddish when mature, and up to a half-inch in diameter. They ripen in early fall and remain attached through most of the winter. They provide food for winter birds and certain mammals. Other names that are used are Prairie Rose, Climbing Rose, Michigan Rose, and Rose-blush.

SWAMP ROSE

These are bushy plants that are not quite so prickly as the above species. The leaves are pinnately compound and usually have seven leaflets. The flowers are 2–3 inches broad with reddish pink petals. The fruits are globose and only about one-fourth inch in diameter. They ripen in early fall and remain attached during the winter. They provide food for a few winter birds and mammals. These plants are restricted to moist soils of our southeastern counties. Other names in use are Wild Rose and Hip-tree.

FLOWERING DOGWOOD
Cornus florida

Dogwood Family
Cornaceae

PENCIL CACTUS
Opuntia leptocaulis

Cactus Family
Cactaceae

PRICKLY PEAR
Opuntia compressa

Cactus Family
Cactaceae

FLOWERING DOGWOOD

These small trees are 15–30 feet tall. The leaves are thin, papery, 3–6 inches long, and have long slender petioles. The flowers are small, clustered, greenish yellow, and are surrounded by four white to pink bracts that are 1–3 inches long. The fruits are red, oval, about a half inch long, and mature in September. They are desirable as food for several species of birds. These plants are restricted to the eastern half of our state where they grow in woods. Other popular names are Arrow-wood, Box-wood, Cornelian Tree, False Box-wood, Nature's Mistake, White Cornel, and Indian Arrow-wood.

PENCIL CACTUS

These plants are shrublike with branching, cylindrical stems that reach a height of 3–5 feet. The spines are few in number but the clusters of tiny, hooked bristles are numerous. The fruits are red, fleshy, many-seeded, pear-shaped, and 1/2–3/4 inch long. They mature in the late summer and remain attached into the winter months. They grow on gravelly slopes of a few southwestern counties. Another name used, especially by Mexican-American people, is Tasajillo.

PRICKLY PEAR

These are prostrate, prickly plants with flattened stems. The spines are numerous and occur three to five together, spreading from their place of emergence. The fruits are clublike, smooth, reddish, and 2–4 inches long. They are many-seeded, fleshy, and are readily eaten by birds or mammals. They mature in late summer. These plants are numerous on well-drained slopes of most of our southwestern counties. Other popular names are Indian Fig, Devil's Tongue, and Barberry.

TREE PLUM
Prunus mexicana

Rose Family
Rosaceae

CHICKASAW PLUM
Prunus angustifolia

Rose Family
Rosaceae

THORN APPLE
Crataegus crus-galli

Rose Family
Rosaceae

TREE PLUM

These are small, slender trees that do not form thickets like most plums. The leaves are simple, 1–3 inches long, and oval in outline. The leaf margins are serrate. The flowers are pink to white and about an inch broad. They appear slightly ahead of the leaves in early spring. The fruits grow in small clusters from very short, lateral branches. Each fruit is yellow to reddish when mature and is about three quarters of an inch in diameter. They are widely distributed along streams or gullies. Other names are Mexican Plum and Mexican Cherry.

CHICKASAW PLUM

These are mostly shrubs that grow in thickets. They rarely grow more than six feet tall. The leaves are lancelike, 3–4 inches long, and grow from stems that are often a little prickly. The flowers are white to pink, about a half inch broad, and appear in March or April ahead of the leaves. The fruits are mostly red when mature, about a half inch thick, and may be utilized for very fine jellies or jams. They are also eaten by several species of birds. They are widely distributed along fences or in old fields or pastures. Other popular names are Sand Plum, Red Plum, and Western Plum.

THORN APPLE

These are small trees with spreading branches. The stems have very long thorns which discourage tree-climbing. The leaves are oval, serrate on the margins, and 1–2 inches long. The flowers are very numerous, appear in April or May, and have five pinkish petals. The fruits are almost globose, about 1/2 inch thick, and are red when mature. They flourish on slopes in many eastern counties. Their use by wildlife, as food supplement, is not as extensive as might be assumed. Other names that are used for this tree are Cockspur Thorn, Newcastle Thorn, Red Haw, Pin-thorn, and Hawthorn.

SOUTHERN BLACKBERRY
Rubus louisianus

Rose Family
Rosaceae

WILD BLACKBERRY
Rubus trivialis

Rose Family
Rosaceae

FALSE GRAPE
Ampelopsis cordata

Grape Family
Vitaceae

SOUTHERN BLACKBERRY

These are low, thorny plants that often form large thickets. The leaves are pinnately compound with three leaflets. Each leaflet is oval to lance-shaped, serrate-margined and 1–3 inches long. The flowers are 1/2–1 inch wide with five white petals. The fruits are black when mature, in early summer, and are utilized as food by many birds, mammals and rodents. Also human consumption of these berries is quite common. They grow in low, moist, waste places in a few southern counties. Other names are Dewberry and Louisiana Blackberry.

WILD BLACKBERRY

These are erect shrubby plants with stems that are covered by prickles. The leaves are pinnately compound with three leaflets. The leaflets are broader than the above species, and less pointed at the tips. The flowers are one or more inches wide. The fruits are black when fully mature, ovoid in form, and often as much as an inch in length. They are quite palatable and are used as food by man as well as many birds and mammals. They are widely distributed over the state and mature in June. Other names are Low Bush Blackberry and Bramble Berry.

FALSE GRAPE

These plants are high-climbing, woody vines that have several features in common with grape vines. Their leaf-blades are broadly ovate, coarsely serrate, and 2–4 inches long. The fruits are bluish when fully mature, 1/6–1/4 inch thick, almost globose, and have 1–2 seeds. They are inedible for humans but supply some food for wildlife. They mature in the early fall and are restricted to banks of streams. Other names are Simple-leaved Ampelopsis and Cissus.

WESTERN CRAB APPLE
Pyrus ioensis

Rose Family
Rosaceae

AMERICAN HOLLY
Ilex opaca

Holly Family
Aquifoliaceae

DOWNY HAW
Crataegus mollis

Rose Family
Rosaceae

WESTERN CRAB APPLE

These are small trees that somewhat resemble pear trees or apple trees. The leaves are simple, blunt at the tips, toothed on the margins, and 1–2 inches long. The flowers are white to pink, about an inch broad, and appear in April or May. The fruits are 1/2–3/4 inch in diameter and almost globose. They are red to purple and have many corky spots on the surface. They grow only in the eastern counties on open slopes, except when transplanted further west. Other names are American Crab Apple and Wild Apple.

AMERICAN HOLLY

These are slow-growing trees that occasionally reach a height of 50 feet. The leaves are obovate, 2–4 inches long and evergreen. They have spine-tipped lobes that are mostly toward the apex. The flowers are small, inconspicuous, and attached by short, slender pedicels, in small groups among the leaves of new stems. The fruits are usually red, 1/3–1/2 inch in diameter, and mature in late autumn. They are consumed by various birds and mammals. These trees occur in our southeastern counties, in moist woods. Other names are White Holly and Christmas Holly.

DOWNY HAW

These are usually small trees, but may reach a height of 30 or 40 feet in rich, moist soil. They have scattered spines that are 1–2 inches long. The leaf blades are ovate to heart-like, somewhat hairy when young, and 1–4 inches long. The flowers are about an inch broad and white to pink. The fruits are globose, red with corky spots, and about a half inch thick. They are quite edible and provide food for various species of wildlife. They mature in September and remain attached until the leaves have fallen. They are widely distributed. Other names are Downy Thorn, Red Haw, Scarlet Haw, and Red-fruited Thorn.

BEAUTY BUSH
Callicarpa americana

Verbena Family
Verbenaceae

INDIAN CURRANT
Symphoricarpos orbiculatus

Honeysuckle Family
Caprifoliaceae

PRICKLY ASH
Xanthoxylum Clava-Herculis

Rue Family
Rutaceae

BEAUTY BUSH

These are shrubs that are 2-5 feet tall and very hairy on younger twigs. The leaves are opposite, simple, ovate, toothed, and 3-6 inches long. The flowers are clustered on upper stem nodes, pale blue and very small. The violet blue fruits are in compact clusters, and each is globose with a diameter of less than a fourth of an inch. They grow in moist thickets of our eastern counties. Other popular names for this plant are French Mulberry, Bermuda Mulberry, and Sourbush.

INDIAN CURRANT

These are shrubs that are 2-5 feet tall. The leaves are oval, with smooth margins, and 1-2 inches long. The flowers are small and inconspicuous. The fruits are fleshy, several-seeded, ovoid to globose, and purplish to red. The fruits are about 1/10 inch long and usually grow in clusters at the upper nodes. They grow in thickets throughout most of the state. Other names are Buck Bush, Turkey Berry, and Snap Berry.

PRICKLY ASH

These are small, slender, branching trees that are often very prickly. The leaves are pinnately compound with 5-19 leaflets that are stiff and glossy. The fruits are about 1/6 inch long, oval in shape, and mature in June. They open in the fall to release single, black, glossy seeds. They grow along streams in our southern counties. Other names that may be found for this species are Sea Ash, Southern Prickly Ash, and Pepper Wood.

WINGED SUMAC
Rhus copallina

Sumac Family
Anacardiaceae

SMOOTH SUMAC
Rhus glabra

Sumac Family
Anacardiaceae

SKUNK BUSH
Rhus aromatica

Sumac Family
Anacardiaceae

WINGED SUMAC

These are small trees or shrubs that are highly branched and 6–15 feet tall. The leaves are pinnately compound with winged rachises to which 9–21 leaflets are attached. Each leaflet is 1–3 inches long. The flowers are small and inconspicuous. The fruits are red, about 1/6 inch thick, and covered with short, acid hairs. They ripen in late summer and provide food for a few birds. These plants are found in dry upland soils over much of the state. Other names are Dwarf Black Sumac, Mountain Sumac, Upland Sumac, and Common Sumac.

SMOOTH SUMAC

These are shrubs or small trees that are usually taller than the above species. The leaves are pinnately compound with 11–31 leaflets. Each leaflet is 2–4 inches long and pointed at the tip. The flowers are greenish and inconspicuous. The fruits are small, red drupes that are covered with short, reddish, acid hairs. They ripen during the summer and remain attached into the winter. They grow in dry soils of slopes throughout the state. Other names are Smooth Upland Sumac, Scarlet Sumac, Sleek Sumac, Shoe-make, Senhalanac, and Vinegar-tree.

SKUNK BUSH

These are branching shrubs that are 3–8 feet tall. The leaves are compound with three leaflets that are 1–2 inches long. The flowers are clustered, yellowish to green, and appear before the leaves. The fruits are small, globose, reddish to yellow, and covered with short hairs. The entire plant is aromatic with a faint skunklike odor. They grow in rocky woods throughout the state. Other useful names are Fragrant Sumac and Sweet-scented Sumac.

BURNING BUSH
Euonymus americana

Staff-tree Family
Celastraceae

STICKER WEED
Solanum carolinense

Nightshade Family
Solanaceae

MISSOURI EVENING PRIMROSE
Oenothera missouriensis

Evening Primrose Family
Onagraceae

BURNING BUSH

These are shrubs that are 2–8 feet tall with opposite, simple leaves. The flowers are greenish and about a half inch broad. The fruits are capsules with 3–5 lobes that open to expose red arils (fleshy seed cover). They grow in low woods of the southeastern counties. Other names are Strawberry Bush, Bursting Heart, and Fish Wood.

STICKER WEED

These are stout, herbaceous plants that are 1–4 feet tall and covered with scattered, yellow prickles. The flowers are purplish and 1–1 1/2 inches wide. The fruits are globular, smooth, three-fourths of an inch in diameter and orange yellow when mature. They are retained through the winter, becoming dry. They are frequent in waste places throughout the state. Other names are Horse Nettle, Sand Brier, Tread Softly, Bull Nettle, Radical Weed, and Apple-of-sodom.

MISSOURI EVENING PRIMROSE

These are sprawling or upright plants that reach a length of 6–12 inches. The leaves are thick, narrow, and 2–8 inches long. The flowers are yellow and 3–6 inches wide. The fruits are dry capsules that have four, broad wings. They are 1–3 inches long. They grow in well-drained, clay or gravelly soils of prairies and are widely distributed. Another name is Large Buttercup.

TRIFOLIATE ORANGE
Poncirus trifoliata

Rose Family
Rosaceae

TREE CACTUS
Opuntia arborescens

Cactus Family
Cactaceae

OSAGE ORANGE
Maclura pomifera

Mulberry Family
Moraceae

TRIFOLIATE ORANGE

These are small, spreading trees with branches that are noticeably green with scattered, long spines. The leaves are compound with three glossy leaflets. The globular fruits are yellow when mature, 1–2 inches thick, and resemble lemons in appearance and odor. These plants have been used as hedges where ample soil moisture is available. In recent years they seem to have become established, on a limited basis, along some of our southeastern streams.

TREE CACTUS

These are erect, branching cacti with cylindrical stems that reach a height of 4–25 feet. The fruits are yellow when mature, almost globose, and unarmed. They are covered by fleshy ridges. They provide some food for birds and small animals. The fruits mature in the fall and remain attached for several months. They are somewhat rare but are occasionally encountered in our southwestern counties.

OSAGE ORANGE

These are trees that are often 20–40 feet tall and have spiny branches. The leaves are simple, oval and 2–5 inches long. The flowers are small and in compact clusters. The fruits are the products of an entire cluster of flowers (multiple type). They are 2–6 inches in diameter, somewhat globose, and become greenish yellow when they mature in the fall. Squirrels are especially fond of the many seeds in the disintegrating fruits. They prevail throughout the state but are much more abundant south and east. Other names are Bois d'Arc, Bow Wood, Yellow Wood, Hedge Apple, and Horse Apple.

MISTLETOE
Phoradendron flavescens

Mistletoe Family
Loranthaceae

ROUGH-LEAVED DOGWOOD
Cornus drummondii

Dogwood Family
Cornaceae

POISON IVY
Rhus radicans

Sumac Family
Anacardiaceae

MISTLETOE

Mistletoe is the state flower of Oklahoma. These plants are semi-parasitic on various species of trees, especially elms. The flowers are small and white. The fruits are globular berries that are white to ivory when mature and about 1/4 inch thick. They mature in late summer and remain attached for a few months. They are widely distributed in our state.

ROUGH-LEAVED DOGWOOD

These are shrubs that are 3–15 feet tall and sparsely branched. The leaves are thin, simple and 2–5 inches long. The white flowers are numerous on spreading peduncles. The fruits are white when mature, globose, and almost 1/4 inch in diameter. They grow in abundance along many of our streams and are fairly common over the entire state. They seem to contribute appreciably to the state's wildlife population. Other names that are sometimes used are Rough-leaved Cornel and Drummond's Dogwood.

POISON IVY

These are erect, bushy shrubs or climbing vines. The leaves are compound with three leaflets. Each leaflet may be 1–4 inches long and is unevenly notched along the edges. The flowers are small and white. The fruits are globose, white to ivory, and about 1/4 inch in diameter. The fruit clusters are small. They grow in moist soils near streams or in low woodlands. The entire plant produces oil droplets which contain irritating chemicals that often cause a skin rash. Another name for this plant is Poison Oak.

RED HAW
Crataegus spathulata

Rose Family
Rosaceae

SOAPBERRY
Sapindus drummondii

Soapberry Family
Sapindaceae

PERSIMMON
Diospyros virginiana

Ebony Family
Ebenaceae

RED HAW

The trees are 12–15 feet tall and freely branched. The leaves are broadest near the tips, slightly serrate, and 1–2 inches long. The flowers are about 1/2 inch broad with five white petals. The fruits are yellow brown until fully mature in October; then they are red. They are globose and about 1/4 inch in diameter. They grow in open woods of lower slopes over a wide area. Other names are Small-fruited Thorn, Small-fruited Haw, and Hawthorn.

SOAPBERRY

These trees reach a height of 40–50 feet and are freely branched. The leaves are pinnately compound with 7–19 leaflets. Each leaflet is 2–4 inches long and lancelike. The flowers are white and about 1/5 inch broad. The fruits are globose to oval, about 1/2 inch in diameter, and usually single-seeded. They are brownish yellow in color at maturity, which is in October or November. These fruits have been used as substitutes for soap. They are widely distributed in valleys and along streams. Other names are Indian Soap Tree, Drummond's Soapberry, and China Tree.

PERSIMMON

These trees rarely exceed 50 feet in height. The leaves are oval, pointed at their tips, smooth-margined, and 2–5 inches long. The fruits are spherical, about an inch thick, reddish yellow and quite tasty when mature. They are several-seeded berries and provide food for many species of wildlife. They are widely distributed on upland soils, such as old fields and roadsides. Other names are Date Plum, Lotus Tree, Jove's Fruit, and Possum Wood.

COMMON GREENBRIER
Smilax bona-nox

Lily Family
Liliaceae

POSSUM GRAPE
Vitis vulpina

Grape Family
Vitaceae

SUMMER GRAPE
Vitis cinera

Grape Family
Vitaceae

COMMON GREENBRIER

These are climbing, thorny vines with simple, heart-shaped leaf blades. The flowers are very small and clustered at the nodes. The fruits are in loose, spherical clusters from the upper stems. Each one is glossy, globular, and about a fourth inch in diameter. These are the most numerous of our species of greenbriers. They prefer sandy loam soils and are widely distributed. The fruits mature in the fall and remain attached into the winter months. Other names are Bristly Greenbrier and Bramble Vine.

POSSUM GRAPE

These plants are high-climbing vines that are smooth and woody. The leaves have large, simple, irregularly toothed blades. The flowers are in loose clusters and very small. The fruits are purple to black and glossy when mature. Each fruit is 1/4–1/3 inch in diameter and has 2–4 seeds. They are quite palatable and very useful for jellies and juice drinks. The opossum as well as other mammals and birds seem to enjoy them. They are widely distributed in oak-hickory woods. Other names are Post Oak Grape, Riverside Grape, Sweet Scented Grape, Winter Grape, Frost Grape, Bull Grape, and Arroyo Grape.

SUMMER GRAPE

These are climbing vines that often reach a height of fifty or sixty feet. They are similar to the Possum Grape but the leaves are more hairy and whitish. And their blades are more likely to be 3-lobed. The fruits are larger than those of the Possum Grape. They mature in July. These grapes are also quite palatable. They are more likely to be found along streams than on hillsides. Other common names are Downy Grape, Ashy Grape, and Blue Grape.

COMMON CHOKECHERRY
Prunus virginiana

Rose Family
Rosaceae

BLACK CHERRY
Prunus serotina

Rose Family
Rosaceae

CHITTAM WOOD
Bumelia lanuginosa

Sapodilla Family
Sapotaceae

COMMON CHOKECHERRY

This is a small tree that closely resembles the black cherry. The leaves are oval, 2–4 inches long, and have sharply serrate teeth. The flowers and fruits are in long, loose racemes. Each flower is white and 1/4–1/3 inch wide. The fruits are first green; later they are black spherical, and 1/6–1/4 inch in diameter. These trees are mostly restricted to low areas of our eastern counties. Other names are Western Chokecherry or Black Chokecherry.

BLACK CHERRY

These are trees that occasionally reach a height of 70 feet. The leaves are oval, sharply serrate and 2–6 inches long. The flowers have five white petals and are in many-flowered racemes. Their fruits, when they mature in late summer, are purplish to black, spherical, and pea-sized. They grow in rich, moist soil in the eastern half of the state. Other names in use are Cabinet Cherry, Whiskey Cherry, Wild Cherry, and Rum Cherry.

CHITTAM WOOD

These are small trees that grow to a maximum height of 40 feet, but often are more shrublike. The leaves are simple, elongated-oval and clustered on short, lateral branches. The stems are often quite thorny. The fruits are oval, black when mature, and 1/3–1/2 inch long. They grow on short racemes with 3–14 at each node. These plants are widespread in thickets. Other common names are Wooly Buckthorn, Gum Elastic, and Wooly Bumelia.

AMERICAN ELDER
Sambucus canadensis

Honeysuckle Family
Caprifoliaceae

POKEWEED
Phytolacca americana

Pokeweed Family
Phytolaccaceae

VIRGINIA CREEPER
Parthenocissus quinquefolia

Grape Family
Vitaceae

AMERICAN ELDER

These are shrubs that are 4–10 feet tall and not strongly woody. The leaves are pinnately compound with 5–11 leaflets. Each leaflet is 2–5 inches long, sharply serrate and sharply tipped. The flowers are white and 1/10–1/5 inch wide. The fruits are in loose, spreading clusters. Each one is purple to black, about 1/4 inch in diameter, and attached by red pedicels. They flourish in roadside ditches or other moist soils and are widely distributed over the state. Other names are Sweet Elder, Common Elder, Elder Blow, and Elder Berry.

POKEWEED

These are perennial herbs that may reach a height of 5–10 feet. The leaves are simple, oval with long, tapering tips and are 8–12 inches long. After proper blanching and cooking, their young shoots and leaves are enjoyed by many people. The mature fruits are purple to black berries, almost a half inch in diameter, and slightly depressed. They mature in August or September and soon drop from the plant. They grow in sandy loam of freshly disturbed soils. Other names are Scoke, Garget, Pigeon Berry, Coakum, Inkberry, Redweed, Red-ink Plant, Pocan Bush, Cancer Jalap, and American Nightshade.

VIRGINIA CREEPER

These are high-climbing vines that are similar to those of the wild grapes. The leaves are palmately compound with five leaflets. They usually become bright red in late autumn. The fruits are grapelike, but not useful for human consumption. Each one is blue to black, about a half inch in diameter, and contains 2–3 seeds. The fruiting pedicels are red. These vines are widely distributed in low woodlands. Other names are False Grape, American Ivy, Five-finger Ivy, and Five-leaf Ivy.

CATBRIER
Smilax glauca

Lily Family
Liliaceae

RATTAN VINE
Berchemia scandens

Buckthorn Family
Rhamnaceae

PRIVET
Ligustrum vulgare

Olive Family
Oleaceae

CATBRIER

These plants are vines that are only sparsely covered with prickles or spines. The leaves very seldom contain any type of spines. The leaf blades are 2–6 inches long and whitish on lower surfaces. The inconspicuous flowers grow in small, loose clusters. The fruits are in small clusters and are blue. Each one is about 1/4 inch in diameter. They mature in the fall and, although they strongly resemble some of our wild grapes, are inedible. They are limited to our eastern counties. Other names are Glaucous Greenbrier and Sarsaparilla.

RATTAN VINE

These are high-climbing, shrubby vines. The leaves are ovate, 1–2 inches long, and have wavy margins. The flowers are small and not very obvious. The fruits are bluish black, oval, single-seeded, and about a fourth inch long. They appear in the fall, in long clusters, where they remain throughout most of the winter. They grow only in lowlands of a few southeastern counties. Other names are Supple Jack and Blue Grape.

PRIVET

These are profusely branched shrubs that are 6–10 feet tall. The leaves are oblong to oval, obscurely veined, smooth, and 1–2 inches long. They remain attached to the stems until long past the frost period. The flowers are white and about 1/4 inch broad. The fruits are spherical, about 1/4 inch thick, and blue to black. These plants have established themselves along our roadsides after having escaped from cultivation. Other names are Prim, Primwort, Print, Skedge, and Skedgwith. Most of these are Old English names.

RED CEDAR
Juniperus virginiana

Pine Family
Pinaceae

WHITE INDIGO
Baptisia leucantha

Legume Family
Leguminosae

BLACK HAW
Viburnum prunifolium

Honeysuckle Family
Caprifoliaceae

RED CEDAR

The trees reach a maximum height of 100 feet but are usually much smaller. The fruits are in the form of berrylike cones. They are light blue, about 1/4 inch in diameter, contain one or two seeds, and are borne on straight branches. They grow in dry soils of hillsides and are very widely distributed over the state. Other names are Red Savin, Juniper, Carolina Cedar, and Pencil Wood.

WHITE INDIGO

These are smooth, stout plants that are 2–4 feet tall. The flowers are white and borne in loose racemes. The leaves are compound with three leaflets that are 1–2 inches long and rounded at the tips. The fruits are legume pods that are blue to black, 1/2–1 inch long, and remain attached during the following winter. Other names for this plant are Large White Wild Indigo and White False Indigo.

BLACK HAW

These are trees that seldom reach a height of 30 feet. The leaves are broadly oval, 1–3 inches long, and finely serrate on the margins. The flowers are about a half inch wide with five white petals. The fruits are oval, bright blue, and slightly more than a half inch long. They contribute considerably to food supply for wildlife. They are found along streams over much of the state. Other names are Stag Bush, Sheep Berry, and Nanny Berry.

DEVIL'S CLAW
Proboscidea louisianaca

Unicorn Family
Martyniaceae

TRUMPET CREEPER
Campsis radicans

Trumpet Creeper Family
Bignoniaceae

CORAL BEAN
Sophora affinis

Legume Family
Leguminosae

DEVIL'S CLAW

These are branching plants that are 1–3 feet tall. The leaf blades are almost circular, but barely heart-shaped, smooth on the edges, and 3–12 inches long. The flowers are yellowish white with short tubes and five spreading lobes. The fruits are curved, 4–6 inches long, and have pointed beaks that split at maturity to form a pair of claws. They are mostly southwestern and seem to prefer old fields or prairie roadsides. Other names are Stink Weed and Claw Pod.

TRUMPET CREEPER

These are woody vines that may reach a length of 20–40 feet. The leaf blades are pinnately compound and have 7–11 leaflets. Each leaflet is toothed, oval, and 1/2–2 inches long. The flowers grow in clusters of 2–9. Each is 2–3 inches long and scarlet red. The fruits are many-seeded, long, pointed pods that are up to an inch across and 4–6 inches long. They occur frequently along fences in rich soils over a wide area. Other names are Trumpet Flower, Foxglove, Trumpet Vine, Trumpet Ash, Cow Itch, and Cross Vine.

CORAL BEAN

These are small trees with pinnately compound leaves. Each leaflet is 1–2 inches long, oval, and smooth on the margins. The flowers are cream-colored and slightly less than an inch long. The fruiting pods are 1–3 inches long, greyish black, and mostly produce 1–8 seeds. They are good sources of food for birds and rodents. These plants are restricted to the Arbuckle area. Another name is Pinch Pod.

OHIO BUCKEYE
Aesculus glabra

Horse-chestnut Family
Hippocastanaceae

SWEET GUM
Liquidambar styraciflua

Witch-hazel Family
Hamamelidaceae

SYCAMORE
Platanus occidentalis

Plane-tree Family
Platanaceae

OHIO BUCKEYE

These plants are usually shrubby but may grow to heights of sixty feet or more. The leaves are palmately compound with 7–9 leaflets. Each leaflet is serrate, 3–4 inches long and 1/2–1 inch wide. The flowers are yellow, appear in March or April, and are about a half inch long. The fruits are yellow when mature, spiny, and 3-seeded if all seeds mature. They mature in the summer and are widespread in our state. Other names are Fetid Buckeye, Horse Chestnut, and Lucky Bean.

SWEET GUM

These trees are large, valuable forest trees. Their leaf-blades are simple and lobed with serrate margins. The fruits mature in the late summer and are attached on long drooping peduncles. Each fruit is a 2-beaked capsule that becomes a dry, globose, spiny head. They secrete a fragrant sap. These trees are restricted to low woods of the eastern half of our state. Other names in use are Red Gum, Star-leaved Gum, Satin Walnut, Opossum Tree, Bilsted, Alligator Tree, White Gum, and Liquidamber.

SYCAMORE

These are large trees with simple, lobed leaves. The mature bark on the trunk of the tree is scaly and light gray. The fruits are globular and hang from the twigs on long, weak peduncles. Each fruit becomes dry and is yellow to brown, spherical, about an inch in diameter, and contains many fiber-covered seeds. They are mostly eastern trees and occur along streams. Other pertinent names are Plane Tree, Button Ball, Button Wood, and Water Beech.

RED ASH
Fraxinus pennsylvanica

Olive Family
Oleaceae

AMERICAN ELM
Ulmus americana

Elm Family
Ulmaceae

RED ELM
Ulmus rubra

Elm Family
Ulmaceae

RED ASH

The trees attain a height of 30–60 feet and are freely branched. The leaves are pinnately compound with 5–9 leaflets. Each leaflet is 2–6 inches long and 1–2 inches wide. The fruits are single-seeded samara that are flattened, winged at the apex, and mature in early fall. They are found in valleys and along streams over most of the state. Other names for this species are Green Ash, Blue Ash, and Black Ash.

AMERICAN ELM

These are large, spreading trees with simple, alternate leaves that are toothed on their margins. The fruits differ from those of the Red Elm because of their oval shape and marginal hairs. They are only about 1/3–1/2 inch long. They grow along streams and are widely distributed. Other names that have been applied to these trees are White Elm, Water Elm, Swamp Elm, and Rock Elm.

RED ELM

These are large, spreading trees with simple, alternate leaves that are toothed on their margins. The fruits are disklike samaras that are 1/2–3/4 inch in diameter and almost free of hair. The fruits mature in May and are quickly lost from the trees to flutter in the wind. They thrive along many of our streams and are very widely distributed. Other names are Slippery Elm, Moose Elm, Sweet Elm, and Indian Elm.

SHEPHERD'S PURSE
Capsella bursa-pastoris

Mustard Family
Cruciferae

SILVER MAPLE
Acer saccharinum

Maple Family
Aceraceae

WAFER ASH
Ptelea trifoliata

Rue Family
Rutaceae

SHEPHERD'S PURSE

These are smooth annuals that are 6–12 inches tall. The lower leaves are deeply lobed on the margins. The upper leaves taper sharply to the tips and have no petioles. The flowers are small with four white petals. The fruits are flattened, many-seeded, and somewhat triangular in form. They are attached by slender stalks near the stem tips and each one is about a fourth of an inch in length. They are widely distributed. Other names for this plant are Case Weed, Mother's Heart, Pick Purse, Pick Pocket, Lady's Purse, Shovel Weed, Wind Flower, Pepper Plant, Toothwort, and Toywort.

SILVER MAPLE

These are large, spreading trees with simple, opposite leaves. Each leaf is deeply notched and 4–6 inches long. The fruits are winged samara and about two inches long when mature. They mature in March or April and soon flutter from the tree as they become dry. They grow along streams and are most abundant in the eastern half of our state. Other names are Soft Maple, White Maple, River Maple, Silver-leaf Maple, Creek Maple, Water Maple, and Swamp Maple.

WAFER ASH

These are small trees that reach a maximum height of 20 feet. The leaves are compound with three leaflets. Each leaflet is oval and 2–5 inches long. The fruits are disklike samara and 2/3–3/4 inch in diameter. They mature in June or July. These trees are widely distributed in woods. Other names are Hop Tree, Shrubby Trefoil, Ague Bark, Quinine Tree, Pickaway, Anise, and Prairie Grub.

BLADDER POD
Glottidium vesicarium

Legume Family
Leguminosae

ANTELOPE HORNS
Asclepias asperula,
var. *decumbens*

Milkweed Family
Asclepiadaceae

DEVIL'S TONGUE
Opuntia humifusa

Cactus Family
Cactaceae

BLADDER POD

These smooth plants have branching stems and reach a height of 4–7 feet. Each leaf has 20–36 oval leaflets. The flowers are orange-yellow. The fruit pods are yellow, 1–3 inches long, and form at the tips of spreading racemes. The plants have spread rapidly in recent years in south central and southwestern counties. The fruits are somewhat poisonous to livestock. Other names are Poison Bean and Rattle Bean.

ANTELOPE HORNS

These plants are somewhat rough, weak-stemmed, and 1–2 feet tall. The leaves are firm, lanceolate, 3–7 inches long and 1/6–2/3 inch wide. The flowers are in umbels. The petals are five in number and greenish. The fruits develop into dry follicles that are many-seeded; they are 3–4 inches long and split longitudinally to release their seeds. They grow in dry soils of open woods or on prairies and are widely distributed. Other names are Green Milkweed and Decumbent Milkweed.

DEVIL'S TONGUE

These are western prickly pears with the typical flattened stems of this species. The entire plant may spread to cover an area of five feet in diameter with some branches reaching a height of 3–4 feet. The fruits are green to brownish when mature and attain a length of up to two inches. They grow in our extreme southwestern counties. Another name is Western Prickly Pear.

PASSION VINE
Passiflora incarnata

Passion-flower Family
Passifloraceae

COMMON GOURD
Cucurbita foetidissima

Gourd Family
Cucurbitaceae

PRAIRIE ANGLE POD
Matelea biflora

Milkweed Family
Asclepiadaceae

PASSION VINE

These are climbing vines that are usually supported by shrubs or fences. The leaves have long petioles and blades that are three-lobed. Each blade is 3–5 inches broad. The flowers are purple to white and 1–2 inches broad. The fruits are ovoid, about two inches long, and mostly yellow when mature, which is in the fall. They are edible and considered a real delicacy in certain regions. They occur in the eastern half of the state. Other names are Passion Flower and Maypops.

COMMON GOURD

The stems are bristly and spread to a length of 15–25 feet. The leaves are thick, bristly, gray and 4–13 inches long. The flowers are yellow, bell-shaped, and 2–4 inches long. The fruits are globose, 2–3 inches thick, smooth, fibrous internally, and bitter. The skin of the fruit is mottled with green and yellowish stripes. They occur along roadsides throughout the state where they mature in late summer. Other names are Missouri Gourd, Wild Pumpkin, and Calabazilla.

PRAIRIE ANGLE POD

These are low, spreading plants with heart-shaped leaf blades. The flowers are about a half inch broad and are purple to brown. The fruits somewhat resemble a cucumber but are follicles which become dry when mature and are pointed at the tip. They are 2–3 inches long. They mature in the summer when they open along a longitudinal slit to release many fiber-supported seeds. They are widely distributed. Other names are Milk Vine, False Cucumber, and Vincetoxicum.

PECAN
Carya illinoensis

Black Walnut Family
Juglandaceae

BUR OAK
Quercus macrocarpa

Beech Family
Fagaceae

BLACK WALNUT
Juglans nigra

Black Walnut Family
Juglandaceae

PECAN

The trees are often more than 100 feet tall. The leaves are pinnately compound with 11–15 leaflets. Each leaflet is 4–7 inches long and sharp-tipped. The fruits are single-seeded nuts that are oblong-cylindrical and 1 1/2–2 1/2 inches long. The husk is thin and four-valved. The seeds are delicious and provide food for humans as well as several birds and mammals. They grow in moist soil, especially along streams. The fruit matures in October or November. Other names are Illinois Nut and Soft-shell Hickory.

BURR OAK

These trees may reach a height of 150 feet and a trunk diameter of 8 feet. Their leaves are simple and have rounded lobes. The fruits are nuts (acorns) that are set deeply in fringed cups. They mature in the summer but are often retained until winter. Each fruit is 2/3–1 1/2 inches long, ovoid, and mostly extend beyond the cup. They thrive in rich soil and may be seen along streams over most of the state. Other names are Mossy Cup, White Cup, Scrub Oak, and Blue Oak.

BLACK WALNUT

The trees are occasionally 150 feet tall and have trunks that are 8 feet in diameter. The leaves are pinnately compound and contain 13–23 leaflets. Each leaflet is 3–5 inches long and serrate on the margins. The fruits are hard-shelled nuts that are about an inch in diameter and spherical. They are enclosed in a tough, nonvalvate cover. They grow along streams and are widely distributed. Another name is River Walnut.

BUR CUCUMBER
Cyclanthera dissecta

Gourd Family
Cucurbitaceae

BROWN SEDGE
Cyperus erythrorhizos

Sedge Family
Cyperaceae

BUSH CLOVER
Lespedeza stuevei

Legume Family
Leguminosae

BUR CUCUMBER

These are soft-stemmed, climbing vines that reach a height of 3–4 feet. The leaves are compound with 3–7 leaflets. Each leaflet is oval or oblong and 1/2–2 inches long. The fruits are ovoid-oblique, spiny, about an inch long and a half inch thick. They mature in September or October. Their seeds are eaten by birds. They grow in low thickets throughout the state. Another name is Cut-leaved Cyclanthera.

BROWN SEDGE

These are stout annuals that are 3–24 inches tall. The leaves are grasslike and 3–20 inches long. The fruits are small achenes that are covered with scales. The scales are yellow or chestnut brown when fully mature. They mature in early autumn. They thrive in wet soil and are widely distributed. Other names are Yellow Sedge, Red-rooted Cyperus, and Brown Cyperus.

BUSH CLOVER

These plants are mostly unbranched, velvety or downy, and 2–4 feet high. The leaves are divided into three leaflets. Each leaflet is oval, 1/2–1 inch long, and may be 1/4–1/2 inch wide. The flowers are 1/6–1/4 inch long and purple in color. The fruits are small seed pods that are oval to orbicular in shape and about 1/4 inch long. They thrive in dry soils of abandoned fields and meadows throughout the state. Other names are Stueve's Clover and Slender Lespedeza.

COCKLEBUR
Xanthium italicum

Composite Family
Compositae

BUR APPLE
Datura meteloides

Nightshade Family
Solanaceae

BUFFALO BUR
Solanum rostratum

Nightshade Family
Solanaceae

COCKLEBUR

These are branching herbs that are 1–3 feet tall. The stems, leaves, etc., have short glandular hairs that give them a rough, sticky texture. The fruits are nutlike, 1/2–3/4 inch long, oval, and covered with long, hooked spines. They are well equipped for seed dispersal and can become quite obnoxious. They are widespread along our roadsides and in old fields. They mature in the fall and may be attached to their stalks through the winter months. Other names are Clotbur, Spiny Clotbur, and Glandular Cocklebur.

BUR APPLE

These are stout plants that are low-branched and up to eight feet long. The leaves are gray, simple, and 4–10 inches long. The flowers are buglelike, white, and 6–7 inches long. The fruits are covered with stout spines. Each fruit is a capsule that is 1–1 1/2 inches in diameter and almost globose. They grow in sandy loam soils and are widely distributed. Other names are Thorn Apple, Low Jimson Weed, and Datura.

BUFFALO BUR

These plants are 1–2 feet tall, freely branched, and covered with sharp, yellow spines. The leaves are simple. The flowers are yellow, bell-like, and about an inch wide. The fruits are globular and enclosed in prickly envelopes which are about a half inch in diameter. They are widely distributed along roadsides and in old fields. Other names are Sand Bur, Beaked Nightshade, Prickly Nightshade, Texas Nettle, and Prickly Potato.

JAPANESE HONEYSUCKLE
Lonicera japonica

Honeysuckle Family
Caprifoliaceae

CHINABERRY
Melia azedarach

Chinaberry Family
Meliaceae

HOGWORT
Croton capitatus

Spurge Family
Euphorbiaceae

JAPANESE HONEYSUCKLE

The stems are covered with short hairs and they climb over low shrubs, fences, and so forth. The leaves have short petioles, are smooth-edged, broad and 1–3 inches long. The flowers are paired in the upper leaf angles, light pink to yellow and 1–3 inches long. The fruits are 1/4–1/3 inch in diameter, globular, black, have more than one seed, and mature in October or November. They supply some food for birds. They occur, as escapes from cultivation, in low woodlands over a wide area of the state. Other names are Chinese Honeysuckle or Creeping Honeysuckle.

CHINABERRY

These are trees that are commonly cultivated but have become naturalized. They are up to 50 feet tall. The leaves are twice-pinnately compound and remain attached until as late as December. The flowers are lilac color in long, loose panicles. Each fruit is a drupe that is yellowish when fully mature. They are 1/2–1/3 inch in diameter, globose, and covered with small corky dots. These trees are widely distributed but not abundant. They thrive in moist, rich soil. Other names are China Tree and Chinese Melia.

HOGWORT

These are herbaceous annuals that are 1–2 feet tall and are covered with silvery green, star-shaped hairs. The flowers are inconspicuous. The fruits are depressed-globose, about 1/4 inch broad, and have about six lobes. They are silvery to tan when mature and, since several are clustered together near the stem tips, they are striking in appearance. Each fruit is a dry capsule that opens to release somewhat speckled seeds (one per lobe). They grow in dry soils over a wide area and mature in October. Other names are Capitate Croton and Silver Croton.

PEPPER VINE
Ampelopsis arborea

Grape Family
Vitaceae

WATER LILY
Nelumbo lutea

Water Lily Family
Nymphaeaceae

GOLDEN CURRANT
Ribes odoratum

Saxifrage Family
Saxifragaceae

PEPPER VINE

These are woody vines that climb to heights of as many as 20 feet. The leaves are twice-pinnately compound with leaflets that are irregularly notched. The flowers are small and inconspicuous. The fruits are green, later purplish, and finally jet black. They are about 1/4 inch in diameter, globular in shape, and fall from their pedicels soon after maturity in early autumn. They flourish throughout our southeastern counties, especially in wooded areas. Another name is Pinnate-leaved Ampelopsis.

WATER LILY

These plants have weak stems that are submerged in water. The leaves are disklike, 1–2 feet in diameter, and floating or are raised above the water's surface. The flowers are pale yellow and 4–10 inches broad. The fruits are somewhat conelike or hemispheric in form, 3–4 inches long, and extend above the water. They contain several seeds that are partially submerged in the fruiting receptacle. Each seed is almost spherical and about 1/2 inch in diameter. They grow in shallow lakes throughout. Other names are Lotus, American Nelumbo, Duck Acorn, Rattle Nut, Water Nut, Water Chinquapin, Yankapin, and Wankapin.

GOLDEN CURRANT

These are small shrubs with simple leaves that are lobed. Each leaf blade is 1–3 inches long. The flowers have tubular corollas that are golden yellow and 1/2–1 inch long. The fruits are reddish brown to black, mature in July or August, and are 1/4–1/2 inch in diameter. Birds seem to consume them as they mature. They are widely distributed along streams and low woodlands. Other names are Buffalo Currant, Missouri Currant, Clove Currant, Flowering Currant, and Gooseberry.

BLUE BEECH
Carpinus caroliniana

Birch Family
Betulaceae

IRONWOOD
Ostrya virginiana

Birch Family
Betulaceae

RED BUD
Cercis canadensis

Legume Family
Leguminosae

BLUE BEECH

These are bushy trees that reach a height of 20–30 feet with a trunk of only 4–8 inches in diameter. The leaves are simple, alternately arranged on the twigs, and oval in outline. The fruits are small nuts that are almost hidden by small greenish scales. The scales (or bracts) act as wings in distributing the floating seeds when they fall. Squirrels and other rodents will eat these small nuts. They are eastern and grow along streams. Other names are Water Beech, Ironwood, and American Hornbeam.

IRONWOOD

These trees are 20–30 feet tall with simple leaves. The leaves are oval, pointed at the tips, uneven at the bases, and very sharply serrate. The fruits consist of leafy bracts and are 1–2 inches long, enclosing a few seeds. The seeds are eaten by a few birds and to some extent by various rodents. They can be found on uplands throughout the eastern half of the state. Other names are Hop Hornbeam and Hop Tree.

RED BUD

These are small trees that have spreading branches. The leaves are simple with blades that are heart-shaped and 2–4 inches long. The fruiting pods are flattened, several-seeded, and 2–4 inches long. They mature in late summer. This is the official state tree for Oklahoma. They thrive in rich soils and are widely distributed along streams or ravines. Other names for this tree are American Judas Tree, Red Judas Tree, and Salad Tree.

PRAIRIE PARSLEY
Polytaenia Nuttallii

Carrot Family
Umbelliferae

COMMON RUSH
Juncus Torreyi

Rush Family
Juncaceae

ST. ANDREW'S CROSS
Ascyrum hypericoides

St. John's-wort Family
Hypericaceae

PRAIRIE PARSLEY

These plants are 1–3 feet tall and slightly hairy. The leaves are deeply lobed or parted and 1–3 inches long. The flowers are in umbels that are 1–3 inches wide. Each flower has five small yellow petals. The fruits are smooth, tan to brown when mature, and are flattened with two separate, winged seeds. They are widely distributed in dry soils of prairie habitats. Another name is Nuttall's Prairie Parsley.

COMMON RUSH

These plants are 1/2–3 feet tall and have stout, three-cornered stems and 1–4 leaves. The leaves are grasslike and 1–3 inches long. The flowers are inconspicuous and grow in spherical masses. The fruits are tiny capsules that mature and become quite dry in late summer. They grow in wet soil and are very widely distributed. Other names are Ball Rush and Torrey's Rush.

ST. ANDREW'S CROSS

These are low, branching, herbaceous plants with narrowly oval leaves. The flowers are on short pedicels that emerge from the leaf angles. Each flower is 1/2–3/4 inch broad and appears in July or August. The fruits are small, dry capsules that are enclosed in an ovate pair of brownish sepals. They grow in dry soils of slopes and are widely distributed. Another name is Common Ascyrum.

ILLINOIS MIMOSA
Desmanthus illinoensis

Legume Family
Leguminosae

BEAR GRASS
Yucca glauca

Lily Family
Liliaceae

SHORTLEAF PINE
Pinus echinata

Pine Family
Pinaceae

ILLINOIS MIMOSA

These are smooth, erect herbs with leaves that are twice-pinnately compound. They reach a height of 1–3 feet. Each small leaflet is only 1/10–2/10 inch long and 1/20 inch wide. The flowers are few to several in number and whitish. The fruits are clustered at the tips of lateral stalks. Each one is a legume-type pod with two to five seeds. They are strongly curved and become brown when mature. They ripen in July or August. These plants are widespread along our roadsides, on our prairies, and beside our streams. Other names are Prairie Mimosa, Illinois Acacia, and Prairie Desmanthus.

BEAR GRASS

These are herbaceous plants that seldom branch and are 2–5 feet tall. Their leaves are narrow, arise near the base of their stem, are erect, sharp at the tips, and 1–2 feet long. The flowers are greenish white, have 6 perianth parts and are 1–2 inches wide when mature. The fruits are dry capsules when mature. They are 3-celled, many-seeded, 1–2 inches thick, gray to black when mature, and open in late summer to release their seeds. They grow on prairies over most of the state. Other names are Yucca, Soap Weed, Palmillo, and Adam's Needle.

SHORTLEAF PINE

The trees reach a height of about 100 feet and a diameter of 4–5 feet. The needles are 3–4 inches long. The cones are 1–3 inches long and remain on the twigs for 3 or 4 years. The seeds furnish food for many birds and small mammals. These trees are widely distributed throughout the eastern part of the state. Other names for this tree are Yellow Pine, Spruce Pine, Short-shot Pine, Bull Pine, Pitch Pine, Carolina Pine, and Slash Pine.

RED OAK
Quercus palustris

Beech Family
Fagaceae

SCRUB CHESTNUT OAK
Quercus prinoides

Beech Family
Fagaceae

POST OAK
Quercus stellata

Beech Family
Fagaceae

RED OAK

These are large forest trees that reach a trunk diameter of five feet or more. The fruits are acorns (nuts that develop in shallow cups). The acorns are about a half inch long, and often are striped, and 2–3 times as long as they are wide. They grow in the moist lowlands of our eastern counties. Other names are Black Oak, Champion Oak, and Spanish Oak.

SCRUB CHESTNUT OAK

These are small trees or shrubs with coarsely toothed leaves. The fruits are acorns (nuts) which are produced in grayish shallow cups that are about a half inch high. The acorns are ovoid when mature, and extend well beyond the cup. They furnish food for a variety of rodents. They thrive in dry, sandy, or rocky soil over a wide area. Other names for these oaks are Dwarf Chestnut Oak, Running White Oak, and Chinkapin Oak.

POST OAK

These are trees that reach a height of as many as 100 feet with a trunk diameter of up to 4 feet. The leaves are simple, alternate, and have 3–7 broad, rounded lobes. They are 5–8 inches long. The fruits are acorns (nuts) that are ovoid, 1/2–5/6 inch long and 2–3 times longer than their cup. They are widely distributed and thrive on dry hillsides and meadows. Other names are Iron Oak, Box Oak, Rough White Oak, Brash Oak, and Turkey Oak.

SUGAR BERRY
Celtis occidentalis

Elm Family
Ulmaceae

WESTERN HACKBERRY
Celtis reticulata

Elm Family
Ulmaceae

BUTTON BUSH
Cephalanthus occidentalis

Madder Family
Rubiaceae

SUGAR BERRY

These are usually large trees with a maximum height of 90 feet and a trunk diameter of 3 feet. The bark is rough and corky. The leaves are ovate to lanceolate, sharply tipped, and 1–4 inches long. The fruits are globose, 1/3–1/2 inch thick, and orange to almost black when mature. They usually mature in September or October and are consumed by many birds. They are widely distributed in dry, gravelly, or rocky soil. Other names are Nettle Tree, False Elm, Beaver Wood, Hackberry, Juniper Tree, One Berry, and Rim Ash.

WESTERN HACKBERRY

These are small trees that may reach a height of 45 feet. The bark is rough with corky warts. The leaves are thick, ovate, 2–3 inches long, and have pronounced veins. The flowers are small and inconspicuous. The fruits are single-seeded drupes with only a very thin fleshy layer. They grow on short stalks that attach, one at each node, in the upper leaf angles. Each fruit is globular, red to almost black, and 1/3–1/2 inch in diameter. They are restricted to the western half of our state. Other names are Sugar Berry and Thick-leaved Hackberry.

BUTTON BUSH

These are shrubs or small trees that are 5–15 feet tall. The leaf blades are oval, smooth-edged, 3–6 inches long, and 1–3 inches wide. The flowers and fruits are in global clusters that are about an inch in diameter. Each flower is white, tubular, four-lobed, and 1/3–1/2 inch long. The fruits are dry, remain attached into late fall or winter, and become reddish to brown. They are widely distributed and may be quite frequent in low, moist places. Other names are Button Tree, Honey Ball, Globe-flower, Box Bush, Pin Ball, Snowball, Button Willow, Crane Willow, Swamp Wood, and River Bush.

PALE PURPLE CONEFLOWER
Echinacea pallida

Composite Family
Compositae

BUTTON SNAKEROOT
Eryngium yuccifolium

Carrot Family
Umbelliferae

LEAVENWORTH'S ERYNGO
Eryngium Leavenworthii

Carrot Family
Umbelliferae

PALE PURPLE CONEFLOWER

These plants are unbranched and 2–3 feet tall. The leaves are slender, smooth-edged, rough with short, stiff hairs, and 3–8 inches long. The flowering or fruiting heads are about 3/4 inch in diameter and restricted to the stem tips. The flower rays are long, drooping, rose purple, 1–3 inches long and 1/8–1/4 inch wide. The fruiting heads are brown when mature and each fruit is a single-seeded, dry achene with a rigid tip. They grow on dry slopes of prairies and are more abundant in our central and eastern counties. Other names are Brown Sampson and Spiny Coneflower.

BUTTON SNAKEROOT

These plants are smooth, except for the stiff bristles on their leaf margins. They are 2–6 feet tall. The flowers are greenish and arranged in globose heads that are 1/2–3/4 inch thick. The leaves are 6–24 inches long and are very rigid with sharp tips. The fruiting, globose heads are very similar to the flowering heads, but become brown in color during the fall season. Each single fruit is 2-seeded and 1/6–1/4 inch long. They thrive in moist, prairie habitats and are restricted to our eastern counties. Other names are Rattlesnake Master, Water Eryngo, Corn Snakeroot, and Rattlesnake Flag.

LEAVENWORTH'S ERYNGO

These are stout plants that are highly branched and thistlelike in appearance. They reach a height of 1–3 feet. The leaves are divided into spine-tipped segments. The flowers are clustered in compact heads that are 1–2 inches long and about 3/4 inch thick. These heads are pink to purple and usually remain so colored throughout the following winter. They thrive on open prairies and seem to prefer rocky, limestone soils. Each separate fruit is a small 2-seeded schizocarp but is retained in the cluster until late winter or the following year. Other names are Purple Thistle and Prairie Eryngo.

COMMON DANDELION
Taraxacum officinale

Composite Family
Compositae

COTTON BUSH
Baccharis halimifolia

Composite Family
Compositae

HAIRY GOLDENROD
Solidago hispida

Composite Family
Compositae

COMMON DANDELION

These plants have extremely short stems with leaf clusters at ground level. The leaves are deeply and irregularly notched, 3–10 inches long and 1/2–2 inches wide. The flowering heads are developed near the base of the leaves and are 1–2 inches broad. They are dark yellow. The fruiting heads are extended by the elongating peduncles. Each fruit is very small, dry, single-seeded, and has a parachutelike set of fibers that serve the plant well for seed dispersal. They are widely distributed but seem to thrive best on lawns where they may become real pests. Other names are Blowball, Irish Daisy, Monk's Head, Priest's Crown, Puff Ball, and Arnica.

COTTON BUSH

These are branching, smooth shrubs that are 3–10 feet tall. The leaves are thick, coarsely toothed, petioled, and 1/2–3 inches long. The flowers are in small heads that are clustered at or near the stem tips. The fruits are tiny achenes that mature in late autumn. They have bright white capillary bristles which resemble cotton fibers. These plants grow in marshes or low areas of a few southeastern counties. Other names are Groundsel Bush, Pencil Tree, Cotton Seed Tree, and Spikenard.

HAIRY GOLDENROD

These plants are stout, hairy, sparsely branched, and 1–3 feet tall. The leaves are oval, 1–5 inches long and have no petioles. The flowering heads are about 1/4 inch high and are crowded near the stem tips. Their rays are yellow. The achene-type fruits are very small but because of their many yellowish bristles and dense clusters are quite striking when mature. They mature in the late autumn and disperse gradually through the following winter months. These plants are widely distributed in fairly dry soils. Other names are Wooly Goldenrod and Prairie Goldenrod.

References

Duncan, W. H., and Foote, L. E. *Wildflowers of the Southeastern United States.* Athens: University of Georgia Press, 1975.

Fernald, M. L. *Gray's Manual of Botany.* 8th ed. New York: American Book Company, 1950.

Gleason, H. A. *New Britton and Brown Illustrated Flora of the Northeastern States.* 3 vols. New York: New York Botanical Garden, 1952.

Goodman, G. J. *Keys to the Spring Flora of Central Oklahoma.* Norman: University of Oklahoma Duplicating Service, 1960.

Lundell, C. L. *Flora of Texas.* 3 vols. Renner, Tex.: Texas Research Foundation, 1961.

McCoy, Doyle. *A Study of Flowering Plants.* Lawton, Okla.: Cameron University Bookstore, 1976.

McCoy, Doyle. *Roadside Flowers of Oklahoma.* 2 vols. Lawton, Okla.: Cameron University Bookstore, 1976, 1978.

Martin, A. C.; Zim, H. L.; and Nelson, A. L. *American Wildlife and Plants.* New York: Dover Publications, 1961.

Shinners, Lloyd H. *Spring Flora of the Dallas-Fort Worth Area, Texas.* Dallas, Tex.: privately published, 1958.

Stemen, T. R., and Myers, W. S. *Oklahoma Flora.* Oklahoma City: Harlow Publishing Co., 1937.

Steyermark, J. A. *Flora of Missouri.* Ames: Iowa State University Press, 1963.

Waterfall, U. T. *Keys to the Flora of Oklahoma.* 5th ed. Stillwater, Okla.: Oklahoma State University Bookstore, 1960.

Glossary

ACHENE.   A small, dry indehiscent, one-seeded fruit.
ACUTE.   Sharp, ending in a point.
ANNUAL.   Living for one growing season.
ANTHER.   Pollen-bearing portion of a stamen.
APETALOUS.   Lacking petals.
APPRESSED.   Lying flat against and pointing upward.
AQUATIC.   Water-living.
ARIL.   Fleshy appendage at the base of a seed.
AWN.   A bristle-shaped appendage.
AXIL.   The angle formed between two organs.
AXILLARY.   In the axil.
BEAK.   Firm elongated slender structure.
BERRY.   A fleshy, usually several-seeded fruit.
BLADE.   The expanded portion of a leaf.
BRACT.   A structure, more or less leaflike, commonly subtending a flower or flowering branch.
BRISTLE.   A stiff hair.
CAPSULE.   A dry dehiscent fruit of two or more carpels.
CARPEL.   A single pistil.
CARYOPSIS.   Grain or seedlike fruit.
CATKIN.   Dry, scaly spike, such as in willows.
COMPOUND.   Composed of two or more similar parts.

CONIFEROUS. Cone-bearing.

CUPULE. The cup of the acorn.

DECIDUOUS. Not evergreen; lost on maturing.

DECUMBENT. Spreading or leaning toward the ground.

DEHISCENT. The splitting of fruits when mature.

DENTATE. Toothed, the teeth pointing outward.

DISK. A ringlike growth in the calyx, or in Compositae, the central portion of the flowering head, bearing tubular flowers.

DISCOID. Resembling a disk.

DIVIDED. Separated to the base.

DRUPE. Fleshy fruit, such as the plum, with a very hard seed-cover.

DRUPELET. Small drupe as in blackberry.

ELLIPTIC. Rounded uniformly at each end and widest at the middle.

ENTIRE. Without teeth or lobes.

FOLLICLE. A fruit with a single carpel.

FRUIT. Mature ovary.

GLOBOSE. Spherical.

HABITAT. The kind of locality in which a plant grows.

HEAD. A dense cluster.

HERB. A plant with no persistent woody stem.

INFLORESCENCE. A flower cluster.

INTERNODE. The portion between two nodes.

INTRODUCED. Intentionally brought from another region.

LANCEOLATE. Lance-shaped; much longer than broad, with the widest portion between the middle and the base.

LEAFLET. A single division of a compound leaf.

LEGUME. A fruit having one compartment and one to many seeds.

LOBED. Divided into or bearing lobes.

MIDRIB. Central vein of a leaf.

NODE. The region on a stem where a leaf is formed.

NUT. Single-seeded, dry fruit such as the pecan.

NUTLET. A dry half-fruit or quarter-fruit.

OBLONG. Longer than broad, with sides nearly parallel on the margins.

OBOVATE. Ovate, but with the broadest portion away from the point of attachment.

ORBICULAR. Circular in form.

OVAL. Broadly elliptic.

OVATE. Egg-shaped in outline, the broadest portion toward the point of attachment.

OVOID. Egg-shaped in outline and three-dimensional.

PALMATE. Radiately lobed, divided, or arranged.

PARTED. Cleft nearly to the base.

PEDICEL. The stalk of a flower or fruit.

PEDUNCLE. The stalk of an inflorescence or fruit cluster.

PERENNIAL. Living for a period of three or more years.

PETIOLE. The stalk of a leaf.

PINNATE. With the veins or leaflets on either side of the rachis or midrib.

POME. Fleshy fruit such as the apple.

PROCUMBENT. Lying on the ground.

PUBESCENT. With short, soft hairs.

RACEME. An elongated inflorescence, the flowers or fruits on stalks.

REFLEXED. Turned downward and outward.

RHIZOME. Underground stems that are elongate and mostly slender.

RIB. A prominent vein.

SAMARA. Single-seeded, dry fruit with a wing.

SERRATE. Having sharp teeth pointing forward.

SESSILE. Without a stalk.

SIMPLE. Not compound.

SPIKE. Similar to a raceme but the flowers sessile.

TENDRIL. A slender and usually twining outgrowth.

TRIFOLIATE. With three leaflets.

TUBER. Fleshy underground stem.

TUBERCLE. Small tuberlike protuberance.

UMBEL. An inflorescence with the pedicels all arising from one point.

VEIN. A vascular strand, especially as these strands appear in leaves.

VILLOUS. Very hairy.

WING. Somewhat flattened extension. Also one of two lateral petals in legumes.

WHORL. The arrangement of leaves and other appendages when three or more are attached at a node.

Index

Acacia: 63
Acer: 42
Aceraceae: 42
Adam's Needle: 63
Aesculus: 38
Ague Bark: 43
Alligator Tree: 39
American Crab Apple: 13
American Elder: 30–31
American Elm: 40–41
American Holly: 12–13
American Hornbeam: 59
American Ivy: 31
American Judas Tree: 59
American Nelumbo: 57
American Nightshade: 31
Ampelopsis: 10–11, 56–57
Anacardiaceae: 16, 22
Angle Pod: 46–47
Anise: 43
Antelope Horns: 44–45
Appalachian Tea: 3
Apple: 13, 21
Apple-of-Sodom: 19
Aquifoliaceae: 2, 12

Arnica: 71
Arrow-wood: 7
Arroyo Grape: 27
Asclepiadaceae: 44, 46
Asclepias: 44
Ascyrum: 60–61
Ash: 14–15, 40–41, 42–43
Ashy Grape: 27
Baccharis: 70
Ball Rush: 61
Baptisia: 34
Barberry: 7
Bean: 36–37
Beaked Nightshade: 53
Bearberry: 3
Bear Grass: 62–63
Beauty Bush: 14–15
Beaver Wood: 67
Beech: 39, 58–59
Beech Family: 48, 64
Berchemia: 32
Bermuda Mulberry: 15
Berry: 2–3, 15, 35
Betulaceae: 58
Bignoniaceae: 36
Bilsted: 39
Birch Family: 58
Bittersweet: 4–5
Black Ash: 41
Blackberry: 10–11
Black Cherry: 28–29

Black Chokecherry: 29
Black Haw: 34–35
Black Oak: 65
Black Sumac: 17
Black Walnut: 48–49
Black Walnut Family: 48
Bladder Pod: 44–45
Blowball: 71
Blue Ash: 41
Blue Beech: 58–59
Blue Grape: 27, 33
Blue Oak: 49
Bois d'Arc: 21
Bow Wood: 21
Box Bush: 67
Box Oak: 65
Box-wood: 7
Bramble Berry: 11
Bramble Vine: 27
Brash Oak: 65
Bristly Greenbrier: 27
Brown Cyperus: 51
Brown Sampson: 69
Brown Sedge: 50–51
Buck Bush: 15
Buckeye: 38–39
Buckthorn: 29
Buckthorn Family: 32
Buffalo Bur: 52–53
Buffalo Currant: 57
Bull Grape: 27
Bull Nettle: 19

Bull Pine: 63
Bumelia: 28–29
Bur Apple: 52–53
Bur Cucumber: 50–51
Burning Bush: 18–19
Bur Oak: 48–49
Bursting Heart: 19
Bush Blackberry: 11
Bush Clover: 50–51
Buttercup: 19
Button Ball: 39
Button Bush: 66–67
Button Snakeroot: 68–69
Button Tree: 39, 67
Button Willow: 67
Button Wood: 39
Cabinet Cherry: 29
Cactaceae: 6, 20, 44
Cactus: 6–7, 20–21
Cactus Family: 6, 20, 44
Calabazilla: 47
Callicarpa: 14
Campsis: 36
Cancer Jalap: 31
Capitate Croton: 55
Caprifoliaceae: 14, 30, 34, 54
Capsella: 42
Carolina Cedar: 35
Carolina Moonseed: 3
Carolina Pine: 63
Carolina Tea: 3
Carpinus: 58
Carrot Family: 60, 68
Carya: 48
Case Weed: 43
Cassena: 3
Catbrier: 32–33
Cedar: 34–35
Celastraceae: 4, 18
Celastrus: 4
Celtis: 66
Cephalanthus: 66
Cercis: 58
Champion Oak: 65
Cherry: 9, 28–29
Chestnut Oak: 64–65
Chickasaw Plum: 8, 9
Chinaberry: 54–55
Chinaberry Family: 54
China Tree: 25, 55

Chinese Honeysuckle: 55
Chinese Melia: 55
Chinkapin Oak: 65
Chittam Wood: 28–29
Chokecherry: 28–29
Christmas Holly: 13
Cissus: 11
Claw Pod: 37
Climbing Bittersweet: 4–5
Climbing Rose: 5
Clotbur: 53
Clove Currant: 57
Clover: 50–51
Coakum: 31
Cocculus: 2
Cocklebur: 52–53
Cockspur Thorn: 9
Common Ascyrum: 61
Common Chokecherry: 28–29
Common Dandelion: 70–71
Common Elder: 31
Common Gourd: 46–47
Common Greenbrier: 26–27
Common Rush: 60–61
Common Sumac: 17
Compositae: 52, 68, 70
Composite Family: 52, 68, 70
Coneflower: 68–69
Coral Bean: 36–37
Coral Vine: 2–3
Cornaceae: 6, 22
Cornel: 7
Cornelian Tree: 7
Corn Snakeroot: 69
Cornus: 6, 22
Cotton Bush: 70–71
Cotton Seed Tree: 71
Cow Itch: 37
Crab Apple: 12–13
Crane Willow: 67
Crataegus: 12, 24
Creek Maple: 43
Creeper: 30–31, 36–37
Creeping Honeysuckle: 55

Cross Vine: 37
Croton: 54–55
Cruciferae: 42
Cucumber: 47, 50–51
Cucurbita: 46
Cucurbitaceae: 46, 50
Currant: 14–15, 56–57
Cut-leaved Cyclanthera: 51
Cyclanthera: 50–51
Cyperaceae: 50
Cyperus: 50–51
Dandelion: 70–71
Datura: 52–53
Deciduous Holly: 3
Decumbent Milkweed: 45
Desmanthus: 62–63
Devil's Claw: 36–37
Devil's Tongue: 7, 44–45
Dewberry: 11
Diospyros: 24
Dogwood: 6–7, 22–23
Dogwood Family: 6, 22
Downy Grape: 27
Downy Haw: 12-13
Downy Thorn: 13
Drummond's Dogwood: 23
Drummond's Soapberry: 25
Duck Acorn: 57
Dwarf Black Sumac: 17
Dwarf Chestnut Oak: 65
Ebenaceae: 24
Ebony Family: 24
Echinacea: 68
Elder: 30–31
Elder Berry: 31
Elder Blow: 31
Elm: 40–41
Elm Family: 40, 66
Emetic Holly: 3
Eryngium: 68
Eryngo: 68–69
Euonymus: 18
Euphorbiaceae: 54

Evening Primrose: 18–19
Evening Primrose Family: 18
Fagaceae: 48, 64
False Box-wood: 7
False Cucumber: 47
False Elm: 67
False Grape: 10–11, 31
False Indigo: 35
Fetid Buckeye: 39
Fever-twig: 5
Fish Wood: 19
Five-finger Ivy: 31
Five-leaf Ivy: 31
Flowering Currant: 57
Flowering Dogwood: 6–7
Foxglove: 37
Fragrant Sumac: 17
Fraxinus: 40
French Mulberry: 15
Frost Grape: 27
Garget: 31
Glandular Cocklebur: 53
Glaucous Greenbrier: 33
Globe-flower: 67
Glottidium: 44
Golden Currant: 56–57
Goldenrod: 70–71
Gooseberry: 57
Gourd: 46–47
Gourd Family: 46, 50
Grape: 10–11, 26–27, 33
Grape Family: 10, 26, 30, 56
Green Ash: 41
Greenbrier: 26–27, 33
Green Milkweed: 45
Groundsel Bush: 71
Gum: 38–39
Gum Elastic: 29
Hackberry: 66–67
Hairy Goldenrod: 70–71
Hamamelidaceae: 38
Haw: 9, 12–13, 24–25, 34–35
Hawthorn: 9, 25

Hedge Apple: 21
Hickory: 49
Hippocastanaceae: 38
Hip-tree: 5
Hogwort: 54–55
Holly: 3, 12–13
Holly Family: 2, 12
Honey Ball: 67
Honeysuckle: 54–55
Honeysuckle Family: 14, 30, 34, 54
Hop Tree: 43, 59
Hornbeam: 59
Horse Apple: 21
Horse Chestnut: 39
Horse-chestnut Family: 38
Horse Nettle: 19
Hypericaceae: 60
Ilex: 2
Illinois Acacia: 63
Illinois Mimosa: 62–63
Illinois Nut: 49
Indian Arrow-wood: 7
Indian Currant: 14–15
Indian Elm: 41
Indian Fig: 7
Indian Soap Tree: 25
Indian Tea: 3
Indigo: 34–35
Inkberry: 31
Irish Daisy: 71
Iron Oak: 65
Ironwood: 58–59
Ivy: 22–23, 31
Jacob's Ladder: 5
Jalap: 31
Japanese Honeysuckle: 54–55
Jimson Weed: 53
Jove's Fruit: 25
Judas Tree: 59
Juglandaceae: 48
Juglans: 48
Juncaceae: 60
Juncus: 60
Juniper: 35
Juniper Tree: 67
Juniperus: 34
Lady's Purse: 43
Large Buttercup: 19
Leavenworth's

Eryngo: 68–69
Legume Family: 34, 36, 44, 50, 58, 62
Leguminosae: 34, 36, 44, 50, 58, 62
Lespedeza: 50–51
Ligustrum: 32
Liliaceae: 26, 32, 62
Lily Family: 26, 32, 62
Liquidambar: 38
Liquidamber: 39
Lonicera: 54
Loranthaceae: 22
Lotus: 57
Lotus Tree: 25
Louisiana Blackberry: 11
Low Bush Blackberry: 11
Low Jimson Weed: 53
Lucky Bean: 39
Maclura: 20
Madder Family: 66
Maple: 42–43
Maple Family: 42
Martyniaceae: 36
Matelea: 46
Maypops: 47
Melia: 54–55
Meliaceae: 54
Menispermaceae: 2
Mexican Cherry: 9
Mexican Plum: 9
Michigan Rose: 5
Milk Vine: 47
Milkweed: 45
Milkweed Family: 44, 46
Mimosa: 62–63
Missouri Currant: 57
Missouri Evening Primrose: 18–19
Missouri Gourd: 47
Mistletoe: 22–23
Mistletoe Family: 22
Monk's Head: 71
Moonseed: 3
Moonseed Family: 2
Moose Elm: 41
Moraceae: 20
Mossy Cup: 49
Mother's Heart: 43
Mountain Sumac: 17

79

Mulberry: 15
Mulberry Family: 20
Mustard Family: 42
Nanny Berry: 35
Nature's Mistake: 7
Nelumbo: 56–57
Nettle: 19, 53
Nettle Tree: 67
Newcastle Thorn: 9
Nightshade: 19, 31, 53
Nightshade Family: 18, 52
Nuttall's Prairie Parsley: 61
Nyphaeaceae: 56
Oak: 48–49, 64–65
Oenothera: 18
Ohio Buckeye: 38–39
Oleaceae: 32, 40
Olive Family: 32, 40
Onagraceae: 18
One Berry: 67
Opossum Tree: 39
Opuntia: 6, 44
Orange: 20–21
Orange-root: 5
Osage Orange: 20–21
Ostrya: 58
Palmillo: 63
Parsley: 60–61
Parthenocissus: 30
Passiflora: 46
Passifloraceae: 46
Passion Flower: 47
Passion Flower Family: 46
Passion Vine: 46–47
Pecan: 48–49
Pencil Cactus: 6, 7
Pencil Tree: 71
Pencil Wood: 35
Pepper Plant: 43
Pepper Vine: 56–57
Pepper Wood: 15
Persimmon: 24–25
Phoradendron: 22
Phytolacca: 30
Phytolaccaceae: 30
Pickaway: 43
Pick Pocket: 43
Pick Purse: 43
Pigeon Berry: 31
Pinaceae: 34, 62

Pin Ball: 67
Pinch Pod: 37
Pine: 62–63
Pine Family: 34, 62
Pinnate-leaved Ampelopsis: 57
Pin-thorn: 9
Pinus: 62
Pitch Pine: 63
Plane Tree: 39
Plane-tree Family: 38
Platanaceae: 38
Platanus: 38
Plum: 8–9
Pocan Bush: 31
Poison Bean: 45
Poison Ivy: 22–23
Poison Oak: 23
Pokeweed: 30–31
Pokeweed Family: 30
Polytaenia: 60
Poncirus: 20
Possum Grape: 26–27
Possum-haw: 3
Possum Wood: 25
Post Oak: 64–65
Post Oak Grape: 27
Prairie Angle Pod: 46–47
Prairie Desmanthus: 63
Prairie Eryngo: 69
Prairie Goldenrod: 71
Prairie Grub: 43
Prairie Mimosa: 63
Prairie Parsley: 60–61
Prairie Rose: 5
Prickly Ash: 14–15
Prickly Nightshade: 53
Prickly Pear: 6–7, 45
Prickly Potato: 53
Priest's Crown: 71
Prim: 33
Primrose: 18–19
Primwort: 33
Print: 33
Privet: 32–33
Proboscidea: 36
Prunus: 8, 28
Ptelea: 42
Puff Ball: 71
Purple Coneflower: 68–69

Purple Thistle: 69
Pyrus: 12
Quercus: 48, 64
Quinine Tree: 43
Radical Weed: 19
Rattan Vine: 32–33
Rattle Bean: 45
Rattle Nut: 57
Rattlesnake Flag: 69
Rattlesnake Master: 69
Red Ash: 40–41
Red-berry Moonseed: 3
Red Bud: 58–59
Red Cedar: 34–35
Red Elm: 40–41
Red-fruited Thorn: 13
Red Gum: 39
Red Haw: 9, 13, 24–25
Red-ink Plant: 31
Red Judas Tree: 59
Red Oak: 64–65
Red Plum: 9
Red-rooted Cyperus: 51
Red Savin: 35
Redweed: 31
Rhamnaceae: 32
Rhus: 16, 22
Ribes: 56
Rim Ash: 67
River Bush: 67
River Maple: 43
Riverside Grape: 27
River Walnut: 49
Rock Elm: 51
Rosa: 4
Rosaceae: 4, 8, 10, 12, 20, 24, 28
Rose: 4, 5
Rose-blush: 5
Rose Family: 4, 8, 10, 12, 20, 24, 28
Rough-leaved Cornel: 23
Rough-leaved Dogwood: 22–23
Rough White Oak: 65
Rubiaceae: 66
Rubus: 10
Rue Family: 14, 42

Rum Cherry: 29
Running White Oak: 65
Rush: 60–61
Rush Family: 60
Rutaceae: 14, 42
Salad Tree: 59
Sambucus: 30
Sampson: 69
Sand Brier: 19
Sand Bur: 53
Sand Plum: 9
Sapindaceae: 24
Sapindus: 24
Sapodillo Family: 28
Sapotaceae: 28
Sarsaparillo: 33
Satin Walnut: 39
Savin: 35
Saxifragaceae: 56
Saxifrage Family: 56
Scarlet Haw: 13
Scarlet Sumac: 17
Scoke: 31
Scrub Chestnut Oak: 64–65
Scrub Oak: 49
Sea Ash: 15
Sedge: 50–51
Sedge Family: 50
Senhalanac: 17
Sheep Berry: 35
Shepherd's Purse: 42–43
Shoe-make: 17
Shortleaf Pine: 62–63
Short-shot Pine: 63
Shovel Weed: 43
Shrubby Trefoil: 43
Silver Croton: 55
Silver-leaf Maple: 43
Silver Maple: 42–43
Simple-leaved Ampelopsis: 11
Skedge: 33
Skedgwith: 33
Skunk Bush: 16–17
Slash Pine: 63
Sleek Sumac: 17
Slender Lespedeza: 51
Slippery Elm: 41
Small-fruited Haw: 25
Small-fruited Thorn: 25
Smilax: 26, 32
Smooth Sumac: 16–17
Snakeroot: 69
Snap Berry: 15
Snowball: 67
Soapberry: 24–25
Soapberry Family: 24
Soap Tree: 25
Soap Weed: 63
Soft Maple: 43
Soft-shell Hickory: 49
Solanaceae: 18, 52
Solanum: 18, 52
Solidago: 70
Sophora: 36
Sourbush: 15
Southern Blackberry: 10–11
Southern Prickly Ash: 15
Spanish Oak: 65
Spikenard: 71
Spiny Clotbur: 53
Spiny Coneflower: 69
Spruce Pine: 63
Spurge Family: 54
Staff-tree Family: 4, 18
Staff-vine: 5
Stag Bush: 35
St. Andrew's Cross: 60–61
Star-leaved Gum: 39
Sticker Weed: 18–19
Stink Weed: 37
St. John's-wort Family: 60
Strawberry Bush: 19
Stueve's Clover: 51
Sugar Berry: 66–67
Sumac: 26
Sumac: 16–17
Sumac Family: 16, 22
Summer Grape: 26–27
Supple Jack: 33
Swamp Elm: 41
Swamp Holly: 3
Swamp Maple: 43
Swamp Rose: 4–5
Swamp Wood: 67
Sweet Elder: 31
Sweet Elm: 41
Sweet Gum: 38–39
Sweet-scented Sumac: 17
Sycamore: 38–39
Symphoricarpos: 14
Taraxacum: 70
Tasajillo: 7
Tea: 3
Texas Nettle: 53
Thick-leaved Hackberry: 67
Thistle: 69
Thorn Apple: 8–9, 53
Toothwort: 43
Torrey's Rush: 61
Toywort: 43
Tread Softly: 19
Tree Cactus: 20–21
Tree Plum: 8, 9
Trefoil: 43
Trifoliate Orange: 20–21
Trumpet Ash: 37
Trumpet Creeper: 36–37
Trumpet Creeper Family: 36
Trumpet Flower: 37
Trumpet Vine: 37
Turkey Berry: 15
Turkey Oak: 65
Ulmaceae: 40, 66
Ulmus: 40
Umbelliferae: 60, 68
Unicorn Family: 36
Upland Sumac: 17
Verbenaceae: 14
Verbena Family: 14
Viburnum: 34
Vincetoxicum: 47
Vinegar-tree: 17
Virginia Creeper: 30–31
Vitaceae: 10, 26, 30, 56
Vitis: 26
Wafer Ash: 42–43
Walnut: 48–49
Wankapin: 57
Water Beech: 39, 59
Water Chinquapin: 57
Water Elm: 41
Water Eryngo: 69
Water Lily: 56–57
Water Lily Family: 56

Water Maple: 43
Water Nut: 57
Western
  Chokecherry: 29
Western Crab Apple:
  12–13
Western Hackberry:
  66–67
Western Plum: 9
Western Prickly Pear:
  45
Whiskey Cherry: 29
White Cornel: 7
White Cup: 49
White Elm: 41

White False Indigo: 35
White Gum: 39
White Holly: 13
White Indigo: 34–35
White Maple: 43
White Wild Indigo: 35
Wild Apple: 13
Wild Blackberry:
  10–11
Wild Cherry: 29
Wild Indigo: 35
Wild Pumpkin: 47
Wild Rose: 4–5
Wind Flower: 43
Winged Sumac: 16–17

Winter Berry: 2–3
Winter Grape: 27
Witch-hazel Family:
  38
Wooly Buckthorn: 29
Wooly Bumelia: 29
Wooly Goldenrod: 71
Xanthium: 52
Xanthoxylum: 14
Yankapin: 57
Yaupon: 2–3
Yellow Pine: 63
Yellow Sedge: 51
Yellow Wood: 21
Yucca: 62–63